Forever Grateful

This Journal Belongs To:

_____

_____

Why Gratitude Matters

With our frenetic, fast paced lives it's all too easy to settle for living on autopilot without any meaningful communication with those who matter the most to us. When this happens, it's all too easy to begin to lose sight of our priorities and start snapping at each other.

When life gets real, you may struggle to express gratitude. That's why it's important to remember the many benefits that you can reap as a couple when you have an intentional gratitude practice.

Gratitude is Calming

It's hard to be angry and grateful at the same time. You might not always be able to choose your circumstances, but you can choose to focus on the positive by practicing gratitude no matter what's going on in your life. Gratitude is calming both mentally and physically, so it makes good sense to make it a daily practice.

Gratitude Gives You Focus

Do you ever find yourself envying the good fortunes of another couple? Maybe they have a seemingly perfect life on Instagram and it stirs up a bit of jealousy.

A daily gratitude practice will ground you and bring peace into your home as you focus on the important things in life, which is your relationships with each other as well as with extended family, friends and community. Your relationships ultimately matter more than any fleeting material thing that you think you have to have.

Gratitude Helps You to Overcome

When you aren't grateful, it's very easy to start feeling sorry for yourself. You might engage in negative self talk such as ""Nothing I do works out. My life sucks. What's the meaning of life anyway?"

Practicing gratitude will help to you to flip the script. Instead of being a perpetual victim, you now have a chance to become the hero of your story, the one who overcame challenges to build a beautiful life filled with abundance.

An intentional gratitude practice can transform your relationship if you allow it to. Here's a few reasons why:

Gratitude is Healing

In long term relationships, it's all to easy to focus on what your partner is doing wrong. This mindset can create a negative pattern of communication that persists for month.

Instead of dwelling on your partner's faults, think about what you love about them.

Gratitude Strengthens Relationships

When you're grateful for each other, it will naturally strengthen your relationship. It becomes easier to demonstrate this without even realizing it. As you take the time to listen to each other, offer to help each other with difficult tasks and make time to have fun together your relationship will get better and better.

Over time, you both will feel valued and heard. This can create a continuous cycle of goodwill that contributes to a more positive relationship.

Your relationship is precious. Spend some time each day letting your partner know how much you care.

We're Grateful For...

Start each day with a grateful heart

MONTH:

REASON:

MON

REASON:

TUE

REASON:

WED

REASON:

THU

We're Grateful For...

Thankful, Grateful, Blessed

REASON:

FRI

REASON:

SAT

REASON:

SUN

WEEKLY REFLECTIONS:

Be Forever Grateful

Smile and Let It Go

We're Grateful For...

Start each day with a grateful heart

MONTH:

REASON:

MON

REASON:

TUE

REASON:

WED

REASON:

THU

We're Grateful For...

Thankful, Grateful, Blessed

REASON:

FRI

REASON:

SAT

REASON:

SUN

WEEKLY REFLECTIONS:

Be Forever Grateful

Smile and Let It Go

We're Grateful For...

Start each day with a grateful heart

MONTH:

REASON:

MON

REASON:

TUE

REASON:

WED

REASON:

THU

We're Grateful For...

Thankful, Grateful, Blessed

REASON:

FRI

REASON:

SAT

REASON:

SUN

WEEKLY REFLECTIONS:

Be Forever Grateful

Smile and Let It Go

We're Grateful For...

Start each day with a grateful heart

MONTH:

REASON:

MON

REASON:

TUE

REASON:

WED

REASON:

THU

We're Grateful For...

Thankful, Grateful, Blessed

REASON:

FRI

REASON:

SAT

REASON:

SUN

WEEKLY REFLECTIONS:

Be Forever Grateful

Smile and Let It Go

We're Grateful For...

Start each day with a grateful heart

MONTH:

REASON:

MON

REASON:

TUE

REASON:

WED

REASON:

THU

We're Grateful For...

Thankful, Grateful, Blessed

REASON:

FRI

REASON:

SAT

REASON:

SUN

WEEKLY REFLECTIONS:

Be Forever Grateful

Smile and Let It Go

We're Grateful For...

Start each day with a grateful heart

MONTH:

REASON:

MON

REASON:

TUE

REASON:

WED

REASON:

THU

We're Grateful For...

Thankful, Grateful, Blessed

REASON:

FRI

REASON:

SAT

REASON:

SUN

WEEKLY REFLECTIONS:

Be Forever Grateful

Smile and Let It Go

We're Grateful For...

Start each day with a grateful heart

MONTH:

REASON:

MON

REASON:

TUE

REASON:

WED

REASON:

THU

We're Grateful For...

Thankful, Grateful, Blessed

REASON:

FRI

REASON:

SAT

REASON:

SUN

WEEKLY REFLECTIONS:

Be Forever Grateful

Smile and Let It Go

We're Grateful For...

Start each day with a grateful heart

MONTH:

REASON:

MON

REASON:

TUE

REASON:

WED

REASON:

THU

We're Grateful For...

Thankful, Grateful, Blessed

REASON:

FRI

REASON:

SAT

REASON:

SUN

WEEKLY REFLECTIONS:

Be Forever Grateful

Smile and Let It Go

We're Grateful For...

Start each day with a grateful heart

MONTH:

REASON:

MON

REASON:

TUE

REASON:

WED

REASON:

THU

We're Grateful For...

Thankful, Grateful, Blessed

REASON:

FRI

REASON:

SAT

REASON:

SUN

WEEKLY REFLECTIONS:

Be Forever Grateful

Smile and Let It Go

We're Grateful For...

Start each day with a grateful heart

MONTH:

REASON:

MON

REASON:

TUE

REASON:

WED

REASON:

THU

We're Grateful For...

Thankful, Grateful, Blessed

REASON:

FRI

REASON:

SAT

REASON:

SUN

WEEKLY REFLECTIONS:

Be Forever Grateful

Smile and Let It Go

We're Grateful For...

Start each day with a grateful heart

MONTH:

REASON:

MON

REASON:

TUE

REASON:

WED

REASON:

THU

We're Grateful For...

Thankful, Grateful, Blessed

REASON:

FRI

REASON:

SAT

REASON:

SUN

WEEKLY REFLECTIONS:

Be Forever Grateful

Smile and Let It Go

We're Grateful For...

Start each day with a grateful heart

MONTH:

REASON:

MON

REASON:

TUE

REASON:

WED

REASON:

THU

We're Grateful For...

Thankful, Grateful, Blessed

REASON:

FRI

REASON:

SAT

REASON:

SUN

WEEKLY REFLECTIONS:

Be Forever Grateful

Smile and Let It Go

We're Grateful For...

Start each day with a grateful heart

MONTH:

REASON:

MON

REASON:

TUE

REASON:

WED

REASON:

THU

We're Grateful For...

Thankful, Grateful, Blessed

REASON:

FRI

REASON:

SAT

REASON:

SUN

WEEKLY REFLECTIONS:

Be Forever Grateful

Smile and Let It Go

We're Grateful For...

Start each day with a grateful heart

MONTH:

REASON:

MON

REASON:

TUE

REASON:

WED

REASON:

THU

We're Grateful For...

Thankful, Grateful, Blessed

REASON:

FRI

REASON:

SAT

REASON:

SUN

WEEKLY REFLECTIONS:

Be Forever Grateful

Smile and Let It Go

We're Grateful For...

Start each day with a grateful heart

MONTH:

REASON:

MON

REASON:

TUE

REASON:

WED

REASON:

THU

We're Grateful For...

Thankful, Grateful, Blessed

REASON:

FRI

REASON:

SAT

REASON:

SUN

WEEKLY REFLECTIONS:

Be Forever Grateful

Smile and Let It Go

We're Grateful For...

Start each day with a grateful heart

MONTH:

REASON:

MON

REASON:

TUE

REASON:

WED

REASON:

THU

We're Grateful For...

Thankful, Grateful, Blessed

REASON:

FRI

REASON:

SAT

REASON:

SUN

WEEKLY REFLECTIONS:

Be Forever Grateful

Smile and Let It Go

We're Grateful For...

Start each day with a grateful heart

MONTH:

REASON:

MON

REASON:

TUE

REASON:

WED

REASON:

THU

We're Grateful For...

Thankful, Grateful, Blessed

REASON:

FRI

REASON:

SAT

REASON:

SUN

WEEKLY REFLECTIONS:

Be Forever Grateful

Smile and Let It Go

We're Grateful For...

Start each day with a grateful heart

MONTH:

REASON:

MON

REASON:

TUE

REASON:

WED

REASON:

THU

We're Grateful For...

Thankful, Grateful, Blessed

REASON:

FRI

REASON:

SAT

REASON:

SUN

WEEKLY REFLECTIONS:

Be Forever Grateful

Smile and Let It Go

We're Grateful For...

Start each day with a grateful heart

MONTH:

REASON:

MON

REASON:

TUE

REASON:

WED

REASON:

THU

We're Grateful For...

Thankful, Grateful, Blessed

REASON:

FRI

REASON:

SAT

REASON:

SUN

WEEKLY REFLECTIONS:

Be Forever Grateful

Smile and Let It Go

We're Grateful For...

Start each day with a grateful heart

MONTH:

REASON:

MON

REASON:

TUE

REASON:

WED

REASON:

THU

We're Grateful For...

Thankful, Grateful, Blessed

REASON:

FRI

REASON:

SAT

REASON:

SUN

WEEKLY REFLECTIONS:

Be Forever Grateful

Smile and Let It Go

We're Grateful For...

Start each day with a grateful heart

MONTH:

REASON:

MON

REASON:

TUE

REASON:

WED

REASON:

THU

We're Grateful For...

Thankful, Grateful, Blessed

REASON:

FRI

REASON:

SAT

REASON:

SUN

WEEKLY REFLECTIONS:

Be Forever Grateful

Smile and Let It Go

We're Grateful For...

Start each day with a grateful heart

MONTH:

REASON:

MON

REASON:

TUE

REASON:

WED

REASON:

THU

We're Grateful For...

Thankful, Grateful, Blessed

REASON:

FRI

REASON:

SAT

REASON:

SUN

WEEKLY REFLECTIONS:

Be Forever Grateful

Smile and Let It Go

We're Grateful For...

Start each day with a grateful heart

MONTH:

REASON:

MON

REASON:

TUE

REASON:

WED

REASON:

THU

We're Grateful For...

Thankful, Grateful, Blessed

REASON:

FRI

REASON:

SAT

REASON:

SUN

WEEKLY REFLECTIONS:

Be Forever Grateful

Smile and Let It Go

We're Grateful For...

Start each day with a grateful heart

MONTH:

REASON:

MON

REASON:

TUE

REASON:

WED

REASON:

THU

We're Grateful For...

Thankful, Grateful, Blessed

REASON:

FRI

REASON:

SAT

REASON:

SUN

WEEKLY REFLECTIONS:

Be Forever Grateful

Smile and Let It Go

We're Grateful For...

Start each day with a grateful heart

MONTH:

REASON:

MON

REASON:

TUE

REASON:

WED

REASON:

THU

We're Grateful For...

Thankful, Grateful, Blessed

REASON:

FRI

REASON:

SAT

REASON:

SUN

WEEKLY REFLECTIONS:

Be Forever Grateful

Smile and Let It Go

We're Grateful For...

Start each day with a grateful heart

MONTH:

REASON:

MON

REASON:

TUE

REASON:

WED

REASON:

THU

We're Grateful For...

Thankful, Grateful, Blessed

REASON:

FRI

REASON:

SAT

REASON:

SUN

WEEKLY REFLECTIONS:

Be Forever Grateful

Smile and Let It Go

We're Grateful For...

Start each day with a grateful heart

MONTH:

REASON:

MON

REASON:

TUE

REASON:

WED

REASON:

THU

We're Grateful For...

Thankful, Grateful, Blessed

REASON:

FRI

REASON:

SAT

REASON:

SUN

WEEKLY REFLECTIONS:

Be Forever Grateful

Smile and Let It Go

We're Grateful For...

Start each day with a grateful heart

MONTH:

REASON:

MON

REASON:

TUE

REASON:

WED

REASON:

THU

We're Grateful For...

Thankful, Grateful, Blessed

REASON:

FRI

REASON:

SAT

REASON:

SUN

WEEKLY REFLECTIONS:

Be Forever Grateful

Smile and Let It Go

We're Grateful For...

Start each day with a grateful heart

MONTH:

REASON:

MON

REASON:

TUE

REASON:

WED

REASON:

THU

We're Grateful For...

Thankful, Grateful, Blessed

REASON:

FRI

REASON:

SAT

REASON:

SUN

WEEKLY REFLECTIONS:

Be Forever Grateful

Smile and Let It Go

We're Grateful For...

Start each day with a grateful heart

MONTH:

REASON:

MON

REASON:

TUE

REASON:

WED

REASON:

THU

We're Grateful For...

Thankful, Grateful, Blessed

REASON:

FRI

REASON:

SAT

REASON:

SUN

WEEKLY REFLECTIONS:

Be Forever Grateful

Smile and Let It Go

We're Grateful For...

Start each day with a grateful heart

MONTH:

REASON:

MON

REASON:

TUE

REASON:

WED

REASON:

THU

We're Grateful For...

Thankful, Grateful, Blessed

REASON:

FRI

REASON:

SAT

REASON:

SUN

WEEKLY REFLECTIONS:

Be Forever Grateful

Smile and Let It Go

We're Grateful For...

Start each day with a grateful heart

MONTH:

REASON:

MON

REASON:

TUE

REASON:

WED

REASON:

THU

We're Grateful For...

Thankful, Grateful, Blessed

REASON:

FRI

REASON:

SAT

REASON:

SUN

WEEKLY REFLECTIONS:

Be Forever Grateful

Smile and Let It Go

We're Grateful For...

Start each day with a grateful heart

MONTH:

REASON:

MON

REASON:

TUE

REASON:

WED

REASON:

THU

We're Grateful For...

Thankful, Grateful, Blessed

REASON:

FRI

REASON:

SAT

REASON:

SUN

WEEKLY REFLECTIONS:

Be Forever Grateful

Smile and Let It Go

We're Grateful For...

Start each day with a grateful heart

MONTH:

REASON:

MON

REASON:

TUE

REASON:

WED

REASON:

THU

We're Grateful For...

Thankful, Grateful, Blessed

REASON:

FRI

REASON:

SAT

REASON:

SUN

WEEKLY REFLECTIONS:

Be Forever Grateful

Smile and Let It Go

We're Grateful For...

Start each day with a grateful heart

MONTH:

REASON:

MON

REASON:

TUE

REASON:

WED

REASON:

THU

We're Grateful For...

Thankful, Grateful, Blessed

REASON:

FRI

REASON:

SAT

REASON:

SUN

WEEKLY REFLECTIONS:

Be Forever Grateful

Smile and Let It Go

We're Grateful For...

Start each day with a grateful heart

MONTH:

REASON:

MON

REASON:

TUE

REASON:

WED

REASON:

THU

We're Grateful For...

Thankful, Grateful, Blessed

REASON:

FRI

REASON:

SAT

REASON:

SUN

WEEKLY REFLECTIONS:

Be Forever Grateful

Smile and Let It Go

We're Grateful For...

Start each day with a grateful heart

MONTH:

REASON:

MON

REASON:

TUE

REASON:

WED

REASON:

THU

We're Grateful For...

Thankful, Grateful, Blessed

REASON:

FRI

REASON:

SAT

REASON:

SUN

WEEKLY REFLECTIONS:

Be Forever Grateful

Smile and Let It Go

We're Grateful For...

Start each day with a grateful heart

MONTH:

REASON:

MON

REASON:

TUE

REASON:

WED

REASON:

THU

We're Grateful For...

Thankful, Grateful, Blessed

REASON:

FRI

REASON:

SAT

REASON:

SUN

WEEKLY REFLECTIONS:

Be Forever Grateful

Smile and Let It Go

We're Grateful For...

Start each day with a grateful heart

MONTH:

REASON:

MON

REASON:

TUE

REASON:

WED

REASON:

THU

We're Grateful For...

Thankful, Grateful, Blessed

REASON:

FRI

REASON:

SAT

REASON:

SUN

WEEKLY REFLECTIONS:

Be Forever Grateful

Smile and Let It Go

We're Grateful For...

Start each day with a grateful heart

MONTH:

REASON:

MON

REASON:

TUE

REASON:

WED

REASON:

THU

We're Grateful For...

Thankful, Grateful, Blessed

REASON:

FRI

REASON:

SAT

REASON:

SUN

WEEKLY REFLECTIONS:

Be Forever Grateful

Smile and Let It Go

We're Grateful For...

Start each day with a grateful heart

MONTH:

REASON:

MON

REASON:

TUE

REASON:

WED

REASON:

THU

We're Grateful For...

Thankful, Grateful, Blessed

REASON:

FRI

REASON:

SAT

REASON:

SUN

WEEKLY REFLECTIONS:

Be Forever Grateful

Smile and Let It Go

We're Grateful For...

Start each day with a grateful heart

MONTH:

REASON:

MON

REASON:

TUE

REASON:

WED

REASON:

THU

We're Grateful For...

Thankful, Grateful, Blessed

REASON:

FRI

REASON:

SAT

REASON:

SUN

WEEKLY REFLECTIONS:

Be Forever Grateful

Smile and Let It Go

We're Grateful For...

Start each day with a grateful heart

MONTH:

REASON:

MON

REASON:

TUE

REASON:

WED

REASON:

THU

We're Grateful For...

Thankful, Grateful, Blessed

REASON:

FRI

REASON:

SAT

REASON:

SUN

WEEKLY REFLECTIONS:

Be Forever Grateful

Smile and Let It Go

We're Grateful For...

Start each day with a grateful heart

MONTH:

REASON:

MON

REASON:

TUE

REASON:

WED

REASON:

THU

We're Grateful For...
Thankful, Grateful, Blessed

REASON:

FRI

REASON:

SAT

REASON:

SUN

WEEKLY REFLECTIONS:

Be Forever Grateful

Smile and Let It Go

We're Grateful For...

Start each day with a grateful heart

MONTH:

REASON:

MON

REASON:

TUE

REASON:

WED

REASON:

THU

We're Grateful For...

Thankful, Grateful, Blessed

REASON:

FRI

REASON:

SAT

REASON:

SUN

WEEKLY REFLECTIONS:

Be Forever Grateful

Smile and Let It Go

We're Grateful For...

Start each day with a grateful heart

MONTH:

REASON:

MON

REASON:

TUE

REASON:

WED

REASON:

THU

We're Grateful For...

Thankful, Grateful, Blessed

REASON:

FRI

REASON:

SAT

REASON:

SUN

WEEKLY REFLECTIONS:

Be Forever Grateful

Smile and Let It Go

We're Grateful For...

Start each day with a grateful heart

MONTH:

REASON:

MON

REASON:

TUE

REASON:

WED

REASON:

THU

We're Grateful For...

Thankful, Grateful, Blessed

REASON:

FRI

REASON:

SAT

REASON:

SUN

WEEKLY REFLECTIONS:

Be Forever Grateful

Smile and Let It Go

We're Grateful For...

Start each day with a grateful heart

MONTH:

REASON:

MON

REASON:

TUE

REASON:

WED

REASON:

THU

We're Grateful For...

Thankful, Grateful, Blessed

REASON:

FRI

REASON:

SAT

REASON:

SUN

WEEKLY REFLECTIONS:

Be Forever Grateful

Smile and Let It Go

We're Grateful For...

Start each day with a grateful heart

MONTH:

REASON:

MON

REASON:

TUE

REASON:

WED

REASON:

THU

We're Grateful For...

Thankful, Grateful, Blessed

REASON:

FRI

REASON:

SAT

REASON:

SUN

WEEKLY REFLECTIONS:

Be Forever Grateful

Smile and Let It Go

We're Grateful For...

Start each day with a grateful heart

MONTH:

REASON:

MON

REASON:

TUE

REASON:

WED

REASON:

THU

We're Grateful For...

Thankful, Grateful, Blessed

REASON:

FRI

REASON:

SAT

REASON:

SUN

WEEKLY REFLECTIONS:

Be Forever Grateful

Smile and Let It Go

We're Grateful For...

Start each day with a grateful heart

MONTH:

REASON:

MON

REASON:

TUE

REASON:

WED

REASON:

THU

We're Grateful For...

Thankful, Grateful, Blessed

REASON:

FRI

REASON:

SAT

REASON:

SUN

WEEKLY REFLECTIONS:

Be Forever Grateful

Smile and Let It Go

We're Grateful For...

Start each day with a grateful heart

MONTH:

REASON:

MON

REASON:

TUE

REASON:

WED

REASON:

THU

We're Grateful For...

Thankful, Grateful, Blessed

REASON:

FRI

REASON:

SAT

REASON:

SUN

WEEKLY REFLECTIONS:

Be Forever Grateful